TO KAKAPO...

This is the third part of the trilogy called 'Poems from Montreal - Night'. In this collection of poems you will see that there are intentional grammatical and poetic arrangement errors. This is so to bring a richer reading experience as these 'errors' allow multiple ways to read the same poem.

I hope you will enjoy these poems.

Thank you

OZ YILMAZ

Montreal - August 2015

A new place

A new place

A new start

Now I am reborn

I am fresh to start new

I wait for the sunshine to enter through my window

Coffee in the morning

Then some cherries on the porch

How can I say more clearly

This is living if there ever was one

Tonight I will dream of a new love

Many happy moments that will sprinkle joy into this house

A tender kiss from a lover

A hug from a friend

Wine shall flow

Memories we shall create

Beyond all hope shall dwell here.

Being me

It is loneliness to be

Too much of everything

To be loved and envied

Then hated

A curse to have more

Leaves so much room

Distance that can't be traversed

Like the moon in the sky

That can never kiss the earth

Fly, fly away

Like the birds in the winter

Seasons change

Friends depart

Leave an empty place in my heart

That is the price of being me.

Butter

I remember when you discovered butter

The thing you detested

Now became your beloved staple

All the while you ate

I watched

Paris just was beautiful

Our windows facing the Eiffel tower

You took your shower gazing upon her

She tried to take you in

But you were the tourist

You loved the butter and the wine

It would have been better if I never existed

Absent man who was just there

Paying the bills

Planing everything

So something could be remembered

I was not memorable

Not loved

A despised thing

I was the ghost sleeping in your bed

A bird drowning as he flapped his wings

Choking

Helpless

Because he had never met a heartless woman.

Comfort

Count me the hours

Until I am asleep

The ocean's depths

The stars at night

Luscious green field's grass

Lull me into comfort

Sing me until I forget

Embrace me till I surrender

Love me until the words are no more.

Crazy

The girl with hot pink hair

Speaking loud

I hear her across the room

Obnoxious people taking up space

They say everyone got a right to be themselves

That is why the world is a mess

Half the people can't even balance their checkbooks

Young are irresponsible

Older ones are frustrated

Slaves working 9 to 5 in a job they hate

Tell me is that who they want to be ?

Somebody got to be crazy

May be it is me.

Blessing

I keep on searching

Through the pages

Through the words

I come up with my hands empty

There are no answers

Unsolved puzzles

Looping riddles

Dead end streets are all I find

Without clear direction

I am a rudderless boat drifting

Open seas call for me

I have no sails

It is only a matter of time

Before the storms arrive

The dark clouds

Stifling heavy air

Big drops of rain

I will just have to weather everything

Stand in a boat

Out in the middle of the ocean in a storm

Who is to save me ?

Who shall be there to embrace me ?

Eventuality is upon me

I pray to the angels

I pray for rain

Soon everything will be washed cleaned

Sun will appear after all is blessed.

Clean up

Now the dishes are washed

All is clean

Is if some storm has moved in

And cleared all the debris

Wide open field of possibilities rests here

New magic could be conjured up

Mixing and blending

Stirring on this stove

Some marvelous enchanting potion could be consumed

We will be celebrating

At the alter of Dionysus

Mortals who have come to worship

Life's pleasures

Share some small part of ourselves

With one another

Then part our ways

Thankful, happy

Full of gratitude for everything

That is beautiful

Elusive as time and love is

We are obscured by the night

Shining as flames of light

Stars... O stars

Under your glorious constellations

We are happy.

And tomorrow is another day.

Birth of Athenas

Insomniac

That is the definition of me

The one who can never sleep

Zombie who walks through the day

Talks to himself in the dead of the night

I am the little monster who scared every women away

I keep writing

That is my claim to sanity

All these words from a jar

Hidden in my skull

They come out

Another poem is being written

It is giving birth

I understand Zeus' pain for Athena

Each night I battle my Athenas

Fierce war goddesses who are killing me slowly

But they are my own flesh and blood

Written from my skull

I am wasted each time

But that is love

An ordained command to create literature

And I return to the shadows of my room to prepare for the next battle.

Desert far away

She gazes into my eyes

I don't turn away

What is she ?

Drawn in ?

Curious ?

Barefoot contesta in my kitchen floor

Her silk dress

Dark hair

A desert far away

Mysterious, enchanting

I want to be lost

And never found

I have found my oasis

And they are in her eyes.

20 July 2015 Montreal

For Gabriela

Cinderella story

Fat woman sits with her daughter

She is brown with ribbons in her hair

An African immigrant man listens to her orders

She is the boss

Created her own version of Cinderella story

With a man who could never leave her

He waits patiently to be sworn in as a Canadian

He escaped hard life conditions in exchange for his freedom

Now she owns him

Please don't tell her slavery has ended.

Dog

My breath is spent

My words lost their meaning

I am the nothing

I no longer can pray for miracles

I have opened my hands to the sky and prayed on my knees

Have I not been faithful ?

Has not been two years ?

Have I not shed enough tears ?

Now, I have no more words

My prayers are done

I have said what I could

Now it is time to bow out !

I am the disgrace

I am the dog ready to die

A dog has no dishonorable death

That is the truth.

Conquests

She catches me in the midst of a conquest

I am the prince charming writing

poetry

She tells me she is coming to see me

What for ?

Don't you know I am the fishnet full of holes ?

I am the damaged good sitting on the shelves of a dusty store

Relics of the past live here

Filled with stories of love and conquests

Losses in love's battlefields

Paradise turned hell affairs

Then... I think I am still here

A resilient worm that just never got eaten by a bird.

Happy man

In the midst of summer

I am awaken to hopes

Warm days filled laughter

Friends around me

Life can be so normal

May be this is all I wish for

Some way to grow old grateful

Memories to have for reciting

Perhaps my poems can be joy filled

Stars can shine ever brighter

I suppose I am a simple man

Wanting to be happy

This time I may even have a chance.

Life after

I don't want to dig up the past

But my dear it is not over

You can walk away

Go on with your life

But you will hear from me

The life you have abandoned

I will be the ghost haunting you

Because I would be there

Above all the failures and set backs

Smiling

There would be little sprinkles of reminders of me everywhere

People will be talking about me

You would not want to hear

But you'd be curious

The man you had said

'You think your life is going to be the same after me ?'

Would be around to show the world how beautiful life can be

You'd know

Your life has not been the same after me

Would never be as good ever.

Life perfect

Church bells are ringing

For whom they toll

Who shall come

Under the sun we are blessed

A summer day stolen

Dreams are made

Memories are etched

Hopes are seeded

Then I can't say anymore

Blue sky speaks for me

Because life can be perfect.

Hope

I keep hoping

That is all I can do

Hope is the bread of the destitute

Counting on a turn of luck

Gambler's pride

Thinking that this is his lucky day

Ha, ha, ha, I am laughing

Because when you got nothing

There is hope

A man dying in his bed

A woman drowning in a river

Human soul in agony

Who is to save ?

In hope we trust.

Amen

Love has not left

Come calling me in the dead of the night

In the darkest hours you run through my mind

You are the ghost of my despair

You with your blackened face

I dare not to look at you

Love you have taken from me

Like a thief in the night

Entered my bed

Chained me to your scent

Flee without remorse

Now I live in solitude

Sadness is part of my daily ritual

I dare not shed tears

To no avail I have plundered everything

Leave me leave me

Let me be in peace

For love has not left me.

Demons

I am faced with my demons again

They are strong

They hold me down

Stifle me

Losing sleep

Worries and stress

Over something which is over

Yet my mind can't resolve it

My heart is heavy

This is not a simple logical deduction

A toxic woman

I am short of breath

My heart is pounding

She has enchanted me with her demons

I am the one to suffer

Price is heavy

She just pranced away

I am the one in the dark

I claw my way

Somehow I am pulled down by memories

Some illogical obsession

I pray everyday to forget

Reminiscence

I am laying in bed

It is 7.44 in the morning

A beautiful day out there

I think of happy days

Festive morning as a child

The innocence

Paris in the summer of 1986

Days before cell phones

I remember simple things

How a man should love a woman

How to fix carburetor

Keeping promises

I suppose these memories

Have no importance today

Soon I will drink my coffee

Look at twitter then face-book

Text a friend

Then I will ride my motorcycle from 1993

At least there a few things left that are pleasurable.

Stillness

Stillness over takes me

I hear but I don't speak

I am the stars and the moon

I am the joy of the bliss

I am the love that you have bottled up inside

I am the lips you have never kissed because you hesitated

I am the stillness within you stirring

I whisper gently

Do you hear me ?

I am the sparkle in your eyes

I am your passion you have never lived

I am your dreams awaiting to be fulfilled

I am, you know,

You very well know now...

I am your voice

I am you speaking.

Life decisions

Split an atom

Be in multiple places at once

Experience joy and Ecstasy together

Sometimes my heart is divided

I am wandering, indecisive

Torn between choices

Nothing is ever black and white

Gray area we call life decisions

Some call it dilemma

What can I call it except an adventure

One way ticket down an unknown path

Some enjoy the thrill

I rather listen to the birds

And write a poem on love.

The need for Bukowski

I needed some Bukowski

When everything is going to hell

Depressed and frustrated

I turn to the pages of his poems

For the most part they are not any good

But they comfort me

Because I could not care less for beautiful words

His language is crude

He just places a single word on lines to fill books

I think he had it good

Drunk to be forgetting things

I have no such luxuries

It is the 21 st century

Nobody cares for poetry anyways

Somethings never change though

Women still want to fuck easy men

Then wait till 36 to find someone to settle down with

Some poor idiot accepts this proposal

Fathers her babies

Probably because he is just as frustrated as me

Not getting any of what a penny less black dude in the bar gets so easily

Women probably hate my guts

Because I don't want them near their shelf time expirations

I rather hope for some twenty year

While I masturbate to a brother fucking a blue eyed cutie in the ass

Then life does not seem so bad

I just read Bukowski

And say 'he had it good'

I will see you up there sometime.

Writing pains

It is painful to write

Each time I dig into my pain

I scratch the surface until it bleeds

Each time I start I fear that I would not be able to complete

It then bleeds more

Redest blood squirting

It is internal bleeding

I rather have a broken finger

Or a cut from a knife

That I can make it stop

This just hurts

Because I remember

I remember too much

My youth on the streets of Paris

Songs of Simon & Garfunkel

I even remember my dogs that have passed away

A wife I was married to once

All is gone

Everything changed

Now I am a stranger in a world I can't call my own

I am the tourist snapping pictures

Seeing too much it hurts

I am the tied up monkey for medical testing lab

I am the cow fed through my stomach

I am the chicken that never sees day of light ever

I am the poet digging deeper

And writing is the only thing that relieves the pain a bit.

Spell

It is full moon time coming again

I hear wolves howl

The clouds move pass with bizarre illumination

I am casting a spell on you tonight

And this is a dark one

I have dug it up from the black books of the ancient sorcerers

It binds you to me eternally

For each time the moon nears full

Insanity shall reign free

Your mind will be captivated

Everything will remind you of me

Everything you taste

Every smell

Everything you see

In every breath I shall be

You shall only think of me

I will be in your blood running free

With each thought I shall grow stronger

You feel insanity roaming closer

All will recall me

All will whisper my name

You see only me

Each word you speak remind you

That I am always with you

I am your thoughts

Your desires

Everything becomes me

For the moon is my witness

Together I have cast the strongest spell

You no longer can find rest

No more sleep

I am in your head

I am in you

I am you

Speaking

Only think of me

For you can't think of anything

But me.

Still life

The story goes on

Life with you is still life

A stale bread

A few olives

Then I am nourished

That is what you are or have been

A nourishment when I was hungry

You did not give much

I did not ask much

I received just that

Still born hopes

They died before they were born

You had been miserable all your life

You made me so too

Then I did not ask for much

Just to be with you

To love you

But I did not ask enough

You gave me stale

Stories of your x s

Impossible missions

A chance to be unhappy

I took them all in

Like they were our children

Because they came from you

They were strange fruits*

You bore for me to write this.

27 July 2015 Montreal

*strange fruit - Nina Simone

Sacrifice

I place my hopes on the alter

Would they be slain ?

Each minute I hear the pandemonium swing in a grand clock

Tick, tock, tick, tock

Time nears

The deed must be done

There are no angels to save this one

She is fierce

Fast asleep

While men die in the battle field

She could not care less

Ismael's knife glistens in the sun

It is the end of July in Montreal

Hopes die one by one

As I write these lines

God's mercy must be upon

All men's failed conquests

For we die one winter day

As flowers wither

A funeral march is sang

From the distant fields

Where hopes once dressed the landscape

Mornings waking up to her skin's sweet smell

Staring at the ceiling while she lays in my arms thinking how blissful all this is

Music sounded better

Food tasted more rich

My footsteps were brisker

But now

A funeral song rises from the hills where hopes once danced

They die like butterflies

No one sees their death

They vanish one by one

I sit here listening to their song.

24 July 2015 Montreal

To M.

Remembering Japan

I remember japan

With manga stores

Colorful billboards

Exotic foods

Dressed up punk groups

Pretty candy girls

Dreamy landscapes

Overcrowded train stations

A thousand year old temples

Artisan craftsman in tiny shops

The yell of waiters in restaurants

Left side driven laced seats of taxis

Endless hours of music of yakuza clubs

Respect of everyone for a foreigner.

Stranger

I am lost in the vastness of the human pool

Loneliness among a thousand faces

Women don't recognize me

Amnesia of senses

I am a strange beast here

People look at me strange

My mind is malformed

High voltage blowing out circuitry

Hulking figure as elephant man

One by one they betray and leave

No bridges left behind them

No amount of apologies can mend

Curse of a hunchback

Contorted mind of a poet

I walk among you a stranger.

No thing

So you have found a new boyfriend

Don't need me around

Happy to be experiencing the thrill of somebody new

How sweet you have moved on

Will not be calling me anytime soon

My number will remain in your phone

Just in case this one does not work out too

I will be receiving a call from you

Asking me how I have been

You will back into your games again

I am your rebound thing

Every time things fail or

When you just need to get your sexual cravings fulfilled

I am just a phone call away

How convenient !

Your not so important solution to life's mishaps

Calling me in Japan

When your father passed away

Because your other boyfriends could not be bothered with details

Always will be your no thing.

Name of loneliness

Does loneliness have a name ?

Did she secretly sneak in

Became my only friend ?

I wait for her to leave

But she is adamant

She lingers on like

scent of a woman in my bed

I could not tell her to go

Sometimes she follows me among friends

I tell her no one must see her

It must be our dirty little secret

She is frigid

She lays in my bed

Not minding me

I tell her we must be through

That she should not come around anymore

She could not careless

I think she is a Libra

Not wanting to talk

But wants me to just be around

So I write while she just sits in the corner

Then follows me from room to room

There is no privacy

Not even in the bathroom

She whispered to me the other day

I am to be her only lover

If I keep up like this

Of course, she is right

Secretly she knows

I am falling for her

And that is inevitable.

Lucky

Sometimes I am squeezed

Trapped in a corner

There I am left with decisions to make

None are easy

Do you sacrifice an arm or a leg ?

Do you walk away from a loss or stay around hope to recoup ?

Between these choices my life is played out

Dices are rolled

But I am not the one tossing them

So woman calls me 'lucky'

Listen... 'You have not been under my skin' I say

She is silent now

Sits across from me fidgeting with her cigarette

Is if she had figured out life

Is if she knows something I don't know

Listen lady, I want to say,

We all are going to die

You, me and everybody else

So nobody is really lucky.

M for Morgane

She sits across from me

Talking about love

For a second I am drawn in

Her blue eyes stolen from the sky sparkle

She tells me of spiritual love with all the innocence

Under the shadows of the night

Rain falling

Time stands still

She looks at me as if she asks a question

Her fingers with rings

Love finds a way to seep in.

18 July 2015 Montreal

Montreal in July

Sitting in a park

Trees and squirrels are my witness

This is my story to tell

I remember when you had inches of snow

All quiet you whispered

'Will you stay ?'

Here we are still together

I could not leave you

Even when you were frozen

Since then we have become more intimate

I have learned to love your wild side

Unusual inhabitants

Strange surprises

You love me in your own way

Even though you never admit

You would always want me to stay

This is our love affair

That is why one of us had to confess.

Love your friend

Com'on give me the best shot you got

You think you can walk away

Walk away

I will never take you back

You are the gambler

Throw your dices

Shake them well

You crave to lose

It is that pang in the middle of your chest that you miss

Overwhelming sinking feeling

There is no one to stop you

You are the architect of your crimes

Go and seek that pain

The immense desire to embrace the loss of a precious thing

You never want another chance so walk away

Feel that sinking feeling in each step

There is no turning back

Don't you dare to look behind

You will realize that you have single handedly destroyed your chances

Alas all good things come to an end

Love... Your dear friend

Queen

Your sarcastic laughter rings in my ears

Cornered in that room

Playing on your computer all day

Then those useless beads

What was your curse ?

Dragging me to your own hell

Reluctantly I had to follow

Point of no return reached

Your madness

Desire to destroy everything

To fulfill your need for punishment

Anger, fury

Burned bridges

Destroyed everything

Until there was no you nor me

We had lost we

Your conquest over

Retreated to your little bedroom

Your mother pleased to have you

Then you think you could have better

Fail, fail, fail

You destroyed everything again

Another man ruined in your hands

Applaud you

You are the queen of masochist personality disorder.

Lost tribe

We are lonely men

Almost not human

Too bad we eat the same food

Consume drinks

Because nothing about us makes any sense

We are the lost tribe of intellect

Picking up remnants of lost values and visions

Nothing is the same

Nothing will remain the same

Changes come in like flood tides

Wiping away everything

The world has come off its hinges

Nothing can fix things

We are passed the point of no return

Apocalypse in small scale

Starving in third world countries

Oil crises in some remote African country

Pirates in high seas somewhere off Somalia

What can we say

This is the new way

Everything is acceptable

Aids, crack, blow

Just the nature of things

You are part of this story

No one has got tears any more

Go on.. Can you sing "we are the world" now ?

Michael has been dead for sometime

Don't console yourself

There is no hope

Leonard already wrote the song

And he has seen the future

We are just playing out our parts

As Elvis said "world is a stage and we must play our parts"

Fisherman

I am waiting on shore

Islands, dark blue sea before me

I dream of your hair

Your smell

The sea breeze moves in

Sprinkling magic dust

Sun kisses me

I remember your face

A past memory

We had them sometime ago

I carry them with me

As sun carries me

As wind moves me

I am standing at the shore

My feet wet from the ebbs

I stare far and I think of how much I miss you

No words spoken over a year

No exchange of well wishes

I am but a drift now

Horizon calls me

I will cast my net for fish

This is how I get through my day.

Empty

I am empty.. you see

I am hallow like a tree

Carved my essence out of me

Burned at the stake

Love in flames of a book

Chard smell of flesh

I am a flame

Empty, abandoned

In the middle of a desert

Rusting

I am the steel of railroad tracks

I am the iron

Beaten by a blacksmith

Torched

Then cooled by a dark pool of water

I am the wine in a chalice

I am drunkenness

Spirit moving in flowing gowns

I am lost

Hallowed

Empty

Thirsty for love's drunkenness

I am crazy to love

For love

I kiss thee.

House soul

Rain is here

Somber, dark, moody

I am back in bed

cocooned up I write

This is it

My prison walls

My sanctuary

My madhouse

House is empty

Soul has departed

Waiting for me to fill it in

Music, paintings, books

Friends and love of things

Smell of food cooking

Moans of passionate sex

Soul will indeed return

Silently

Shy, graceful

She will sneak in between these rooms

And kiss me good night.

Filming

We are filming

In a basement somewhere in nowhere

There is a stench

Air is stuffy

I inhale

I am thinking would I be sick

This scene we must get

I recite my lines looking tough

I am the monster

Kneeling before a murdered body

May be just may be

I touch a soul

All this will be worth the pain.

Drive

Drive, drive

On open roads

Traffic jams

Beside big trucks

We are rolling to discover

Caged in cars

Looking for our freedom

Searching for our lost care free youth again.

Dinner guests

Hour ticks away

Soon guests will come in

Then we must begin

Preparations, cooking

Wine flowing

All this will be remember fondly

Everyone will dine

Women will be happy

We will talk

Until everyone has had their fill

Then it will be late

Everyone will leave

I will lay down on my bed

Promise myself that this would all be good

My eyes will be heavy

My mother will be watching me

Probably saying

'Son, you have done good.'

She will be there to receive me.

How

She is out of place

Nose ring

White platinum hair

Ring on eight fingers

She listens

I talk a little

I ask she answers

Excuse me but

This is highly unusual for me !

She sees something others don't see

Who is she ?

A friend of a friend

We sit in the car

She is curious

I am fine being here

We could drive to New York

I told her I wish I could write a poem about her

But I don't know you

You puzzle me

An ending box openings

Why are you wired differently ?

What are your books ?

What do you sing for me ?

How soft are your lips ?

Architect

She is at the other end of the world

Somehow she is still there

After all we have been through

In her own way she creates her heaven

This, that plus the additions

She is the architect of her world

Constructing livable habitat

Yet I am there

Far away

But still there

Like a star in dark sky

Shining

Ever present

And I am thankful because

She sees my light.

22 July 2015 Montreal

For Bahar

Complicated beings

She calls me up

A simple bike ride it is suppose to be

But nothing is simple

When a woman wraps her arms around a man

The wind speaks in whispers

Sun kisses upon lips

Engine screams 'more please'

Men and women are complicated beings

Best when things are left unsaid.

Alien

They come sit in my terrace

These two girls speaking about men

I serve seafood risotto and white wine

I am in a foreign land

Alien among women

I only look human

She talks of men in uniforms

How Jamaican men can be sexy

I am deciphering hieroglyphics

Have you heard of adagio or Bach's cello suite ?

They are playing in my head

As she recites her lines

I am receiving Morse code

I hear everything is sunny down there

Aegean sea must be so beautiful this time of the year

Something must have been confused

I am still working on algorithms

You must have send me some javascript

Were we talking about java coffee

I can't remember

There must have been some confusion

Because I am not from this planet.

Battle

I hear St.Louis Infirmary

Let her go, let her go

Have you ever cut yourself on purpose

Severed an arm

Killed something precious

Have you ever been merciless ?

Have you died and risen like Lazarus ?

She is dead

I am among the living

The song is in my head

The battle rages on

It is a blissful sunny afternoon

Not even the leaves make a move

I hear the clash of blades

The screams of dying men

Angels are too busy

Taking men up to heaven

They died for love

They never lived for love

Their amours are sheet metal

Pierced !

St.Louis Infirmary it is

A funeral march for a woman long dead

No burial here

She is lost in the past

Behind the facade of pretense.

As good as it gets

My eyes close

And I am hungry

Everything comes together

I am naked in bed

Saturday mornings are like this

Waking up alone in a king size bed

Ceilings are pure white

Light streams through the openings of the curtains

I will soon leave my bed and work

That is how I escape loneliness

Poems will be formed in my head

Because these emotions disturb me

May be one day I wake to sound of my children

To the smell of pancakes

A tender kiss from the woman I made love to the night before

Until then this is as good as it gets.

Bukowski's death

Good God,

What happened to the man I used to read ?

I picked up a Bukowski from my library

'New Poems' it says

He could not write a good poem at his old age

I patiently read each line

Hoping I see something worth under lining

Pure waste on paper printed

All the while thinking how I am going to get rid of this book

I need more space in my shelves

The man just got old

He could not write

I suppose even our heroes die.

Liberty

What can I tell you at 3.20 in the morning ?

We have been together

You and I

We have never managed to work things through

You keep laying in my bed asleep

But your presence disturbs me

Don't you know your ghosts are not welcome here anymore ?

Go on set yourselves free

Haunt your mistress now

I have had you as unwanted guests for far too long

Now we must cut ties

Severe all relationship

Our love has become a wall ornament

A story to be told after too much wine drinking

Remembered fondly as tender pain that has left it is scar in the deepest places

Now it is healed

So your ghosts can't be here

They have no place

Angels guard me instead

My prayers are of gratitude

For the divine intervention

Thank you, thank you

Heavenly Father

I have been liberated.

Fragile men

We become fragile as men

Sensitive, caring, hoping

We lose our outer skin

Become weakened by our humanity

Too much to hold within us

Things just boil over

Stories, wisdom, love

These are dangerous things

Makes us caring

Broken promises, lies, pretension

Disappointments

They make us fragile,

Very fragile

As a twig,

A bird singing,

People just snap them

Women take out shotguns and silence them

We hold on to hope

Write, write, write

Because this is the only way to deal with reality

In the end reality kills us all

One by one

Rilke, Nietzsche, Hemingway,

You, me and a few still on the way.

Indecisive victory

Just when I think it is over

Another matter needs my attention

I work through all this

Completion nears

Then it is something else

We need our own victory I say

But it is to no avail

I get what I get

I hear "take it and like it" being said to Humphrey Bogart

This is how things are around here

We just get what we can

Hope to live through disappointments

In the mean while I search for my own

Lauren Bacall

I too want to have children

I am old but hopeful.

Green eyes

She looks at me with green eyes

Her words are well chosen

Every thought goes through a strainer

She can't say anything

We are just friends

The other side is unchartered territory

A point of no return can't be crossed

How can she say what is on her mind

Instead she is hoping that I catch on

I can't traverse the boundless oceans that separates us

We are the great lake swimmers

Scared of the bottom covered green

There are no monsters lurking beneath

Just we got our demons in our pitiless abyss

Instead we are bound for unknown destinations

Our partners are foreign

We are strangers to each others bodies

Friends we shall remain.

Grand comedy

Think not you are safe

That you have been given a break

You are walking on a tight rope

The bridge of Si-rat

You can fall any time

Let your foot slip

Loose your balance

Or just slide

Because you are a sinner

Jut like me

That is why we are blessed

Living under the grace of God

Kiss the sky

Bow down

Be humbled by the beauty

It is a never ending cycle

You too are a good doer

However small your deeds are

Open your arms

Embrace your gift

Love, love

The grand comedy

For you are the actor

And the acted upon

Your laughter will echo

Beyond time.

Herem

She is dead

Her beautiful white body stretched out on her bed

She sleeps now eternally

Her soul has departed

She won't be among us

A ghost that is invisible

Her voice will be heard

Her presence felt

We will discounted as the mumblings of someone we knew once

Now... not among us

She will attempt to reach me

From the great beyond

She does not know once dead

There is no return among the living

She will march on

There would be a mirage of her leaving

Disappearing into the night

Herem a toi !

Herem a toi !

25 July 2015 Montreal

For M.

Inevitability

I am in the dark now

Waiting

A tiger cornered

Ready to pounce

It is the waiting that is killing me

Hours turned days

No news of you I wait

Time keeps ticking

In no one's favor

But I have taken my guard

If I come out of this victorious

That is when I will speak

So much to do

To write and more

One day when everything has come together

I can say I persevered

Until then I will keep quiet

Hide in my corner

Preparing

Because inevitability

Comes knocking on everyone's door

That includes you my dear.

Experiments

Girl with a nose ring

She tells me she is experimenting with drugs

Wants to expand her mind

Life can be so limiting sometimes

Caged, cornered, helpless

People are ready to do anything in Desperation

Can I tell her we live in the age of meritocracy ?

Average intelligence can go a long way

Why be the outcast, the unwanted ?

Just march with the sheep

Pretend you are happy among them

Save your efforts

Die while you still have a chance

At the age of 80

No one will ever miss you.

Nothing

She stares at me without blinking

Her eyes wide open

Tapping on a telegraph knob

Somethings does not register

Words are omitted

Sentences are passed through a blender

Nothing is ever complete

Nothing all makes sense

She drinks her second beer

This is nothing

She smells of whiskey at 10 in the morning

Believe me

There is a can of worms under that skin.

More than love

It is just not there

The love you said you would give

All was a lie

A facade of pretension

Your search to find someone to love

A happy home

Nothing accomplished in your years

A woman of solitude

Bent to self inflicted pain

Destruction of all good in her life

I must admit

I am the fool

The man who stood up to say

I will be your dream

Hypocrite who said one thing

Wished to have men who could deliver pain

I count on time

There will be a story tell

A woman who made all her fears a reality

Destitute, poverty and loneliness

A perfect hell

She secretly wished for

Because she loved pain more than love.

Ma ville

I am on top of a hill

Montreal beneath my feet

I gaze far and there is no end

It is everything under the bluest sky

My ville with restaurants & cafes

Friends, talented people

I am amongst you

Part of everything

Deep down I know I belong to you

You have taken me in

Unknowingly I have fallen in love with you

Through your streets I have walked to find myself

In your coldest winters I have entered the warmest hearts

I am yours

You are mine

Eloped we are

Embrace me in your bosom eternally.

Red

I flip the table

Anger over takes me

I am the race car driver

In dark green Jaguar

Engine revs

I see red

Red line has been crossed

Gas pedal has hit the floor

There is no slowing down now

I am the dare devil

I am the one screaming

'Com'on.. Give me your best shot'

I am unstoppable

Adrenaline rush courses in my veins

What a thrill !

What a thrill !

I see red

And she is wearing stilettos.

Remains

It is a hot day in august

Air sits heavy

I think of the past

Bodrum may be Çesme

Somewhere innocence ran free

When I could believe in you with naivety of a child

Before the clouds moved in

Could it be the summer of 1946 ?

I hear the sirens going mad

Another bombing raid

Nothing on the horizon

Could I be mistaken ?

Were we not happy ?

Did I loose an arm or a leg in the battle

Suffering from amnesia ?

How did all this happen ?

I am awaken thousands of miles away in Canada

I see we are blown to pieces

Not a trace remains.

Songs of Muses

The band keeps playing

It is a warm summer day in July

Sweet scent of music is in the air

I hear the call of the bees

Wings of butterflies chirping

My heart takes flight in the rhythm

I am lost in your love

Songs of Muses ring in my ears

Have I been summoned by Sirens ?

Do I follow you my dear

Where no two hearts have gone before ?

Love, love, love deeply

It is the call of eternity.

Shame

Shame on you death

A Cuban cigar in my hand

LVB porto beside me

I hear Ibrahim Ferrer singing

How can death ask for a life ?

If today is a moment of contentment

How can I say I am sorry to have lived ?

Has not your kiss poisoned me ?

Are you not in my veins running ?

I have loved

How can I lament for the heartache ?

If I can't embrace you

Then let me be glad for our days of togetherness

If death is to be

Let it be sweet like your kiss.

Silence of the night

It is that time of the night again

When silence falls upon everything

Then it is just me alone

Words come to me

Like silent visitors that drop their offerings into my well

There I gather them for a storm

I stir and make winds

One by one I send them forth like arrows from a bow

Each cast from my heart's yearnings

Each loved and caressed

These lines quench the thirst of my unfulfilled desires

Each uttering is a call for hope

What then can I say to the night

But come in silence and be my lover till dawn.

The burden of the gift

From anger comes the words

From frustration comes the spirit

From loneliness comes the emotions

I carry the burden

I alone endure the agony for these words

Crucified by love's fire

I bear my wounds open

They are never to heal

They belong to humanity

For every man who has been scorned

For every woman abandoned

In the midst of a love affair

I am the sacrificial lamb at God's alter

For everything human

For the failures and triumphs

We endure in rediscovering ourselves

I am here to tell your stories

I am the mute among you

Whispering through my silent wails

Suffering through these lines

For I am the one with the burden of the gift

I bear open my bosom as a shield

Hear me, O hear me beloved soul

For these words are not mine

They are yours

Sent to you through me.

Squirrel in the porch

There is a squirrel in my porch

My first house guest

May be I am the guest around here

I just moved in

Taking up space

We must learn to get along

Me with my books

Our silent sitting sessions

We have a long winter coming

We may need each other

Come by to visit me

I long for a friend.

Madness by intoxication

She is in the sunshine streaming through the window

She is in the music

She is the warmth I feel in the air

She seeps under my skin

Intoxicated I slowly got mad

The scent I can't forget

I breath the air

Nothing can stop me

I am running against the breeze

Wind caresses my hair

I feel you beneath everything

You are the air I breath

I am intoxicated in this madness

Fly, fly,

I am the bird in the sky

My feet will never touch the ground

I have been intoxicated by love.

The actor

He sits at the hotel lobby

His shoes dirty

Penny-less, listless

He drifts

A pretty face

Women just love

Because he fits the bill

He is an actor without a role

No producer to call his own

A woman just waits for him

She is hopeful that he makes it

Not knowing he would just move on

That is life

A pretty face gets you by

Lucky with the ladies

Glorious brouhaha behind a facade

That pretty much does nothing.

Gift of a poet

There is a lot of Leonard Cohen's words in my ears

I hear Suzanne, So Long Marianne, Famous Blue Rain Coat

In each I find dedication of a song to a break up

A woman who has left her mark

That is why I can write today

My days filled with joy carving deep marks hollowed by a break up

In those crevices drops of inspiration gather

Words well up

Then I harvest them

Delicately, gently

Because they are gifts from the heavens

Here I say

Here it is my contribution to life

From my pains I have made

Beautiful...

I share them with you.

Love...

Your dear poet.

Rockstar God

She awaits me

Insanity

She awaits like she has awaited many

Then there is death

He is more welcoming

When it comes to a matter of choice death is safer

People will shake their heads

And some will say he was a great man

He wrote so many wonderful things

Only a few would understand the weight, the burden, the wrestle with insanity

It is always the sane people who could survive

Look at Nietzsche

He did not have a very good ending

Hemingway chose the safe way out

I always wondered if the women in my life ever would miss me

Would they say 'he was the best or the worst thing that ever happened to me'

Because I never would want to be an ordinary love affair

I want to be the insanity

I want to be dancing with death

Have kiss from the heavens

And disappear like a Rockstar God before my time.

Worshipers

Light dimmed low

We are gathered for our worship

Music moves our feet

Lights flashing

We become mesmerized

Surrender ourselves to the rhythm

We are here to worship the divine inside

As we move in our fashion

Gathered to experience something beyond reality

Our hearts open up to love

Merge with all

We are the worshipers of our divine selves

All our answers are within us

Everything begins here

We are beyond time and reality

Experiencing the love with our beings

Come embrace me

You were a stranger, an enemy

Now we are brothers and sisters on the same path

Love, love, love me all

As I give so shall you receive

We kiss the eternal

Melt into each others souls.

Violins in fortissimo

Adagio plays on

Violins in fortissimo

There is love

I understand Van Gogh

Why he cut off his ear !

World opens up to me

I am engulfed in a quick sand

I disappear into the bosom of everything

Sound of everything

Violins in fortissimo

Heart break

Love crushed

Violins fortissimo

They return

There is hope for tomorrow.

Wakefulness

Past 4 am

I am going to sleep good tonight

Because I left wakefulness

She was the one who ruled my day

Let me see life under the sun

Now she is widowed

I no longer life among the living

I am a ghost sliding through time

A whisper faintly in the wind

I am your parched lips from the salt of the Mediterranean sea

I too love you

Although we never met

You are there in the possibility of time

I kiss you and reality ceases to exist

Only because I love you

For this I could not sleep

There is a sofa in the living room

Where I will go lay down to die

Because I have seen the light.

Exile

I am stranded

Lost in a continent

I suppose this is called pain

Loneliness, struggle, exile

I am just waiting

I have made a choice

Now there is no going back

A fight for survival

A desire to live

With pain or without remorse

However it may be

I miss the bosom of my mother

Love of my lover

It is called loneliness

No, I am not bitter

This life teaching me to live again.

Observer

There is a pause during the day

I hear and see things

Spanish spoken by two girls at the other table

The stale smoked meat on my plate

Some cheap commercial coffee I keep drinking

This is it

This is the moment I see and hear things

I am intimate with the beautiful and ugly

I just let them sit at my table

They give me their versions of their stories

I write them down diligently

I know this is as close to life anyone gets

Intimate, insane, in love with the chaos

For a moment all the suffering makes sense

All the beauty just blends in

She is just beautiful

And I am the observer

Taking notes.

Some souls

I keep calling you

My mind is spinning

You have no heart

All that the universe offers

Prayers and hopes

Fall on deaf ears

Life is frozen

Love is mute

You are heartless

A mutant twisted

Nothing pierces through your skin

Hallow empty dead space

An abyss where everything disappears

No angel trespasses your darkness

No hope lives in your domain

All is frozen in your emptiness

Mortals have fallen

Love is slain at your alter

Pain rules in your sphere

You seek fulfillment in solitude

Yet all is futile

Darkness covers your sky

Where no light of hope can penetrate

Alas some souls have no redemption

Because they have killed everything inside.

Slow death

You kill me

But slowly

In a very sadistic way

Tormenting me with memories

Things I no longer can have

You take hope away

Very slowly

Day by day

There is more distance between us

I know we must grow a part

That is the slow death I am talking about

The ones I see us withering away

No more us

Just memories

That is why dying makes sense

Slowly

Excruciatingly slowly

Minute by minute

Day by day

You growing old

Me wasting away

I leave this behind

A homage of my love to you.

Mess

I keep looking blankly at everything

I am lulled into a state of quiet observance

Is it a funeral gathering

A solemn promise of silence

Still air hanging in the room after a quarrel

It is a forest fire

Heat turned down

Sound muted

Fire spreads

Everything is engulfed

My brain is overwhelmed

I can't think straight

No, I must not panic

Just be still

While the fire engulfs everything

Love burns to ashes

Old photographs cast into the flames

Memories vanish one by one

You are gone too

Disappeared into the darkness

Now only the stillness remains

Soon all will be pitched black

I will sit there in utter darkness

Trying to make sense of this mess.

Escapade

She just appeared out of nowhere

A woman in a small town

Surrounded by all the familiar people

A child, a car, a job

She is that

A life with perfectly defined edges

Now she would venture off

Seeking some kind of adventure

A man like me has mystery

A poet, a writer in a tiny apartment in the city

I would talk about wine

Cook some amazing things

A change of scenery

She would be well content I think

Safe, away from everything

An escapade she can handle

Each night she return home

Driving 45 minutes each way

She will be thinking about all this

The excitement, romance

A get away made perfectly for her.

Nightmare

A violent nightmare

I am awaken breathless

Old me is dead

Skull crushed

Remnants disposed

I have no reference

He has been gone for sometime

Can the old me be dead ?

Disposed for good ?

What happens to this man now ?

Questions linger on

But possibilities remain

Something amazing can be born

Out of the ashes of the past

I could be made new

Free, happy, complete.

Questions

Tired,

Time ticks 2 am

This is it

The final call for the day

Before I forget everything

Turn a blind eye to reality

Much has been hanging in the air

The love unresolved

Confusion un dealt

Unanswered questions remain

What more can I say but

Surrender to the night peacefully.

Rain

Time creeps past mid night

Tonight I have rain as my guest

Bringing back memories

Paris in the fall

I remember a small park on 23 rd street in New York

I used to walk my dog there

She is long gone now

Amsterdam with all her glory of canals and my bike

That too is far now

Buenos Aires

Mi querido Buenos Aires

Streets of Palermo

Milongas till 4 am

Istanbul with its misery

How beautiful Bebek looked

Turquoise colors of Bosphorous

Rain is kind

Nourishing earth

Bearing gifts of memories

She sometimes stays through the night

My secret lover.

Ordinary

Ordinary bores me

I detest meritocracy

Yet I live a world built up on it

Lifeless souls inhabiting buildings

Crowding the streets

Women in mini skirts

Bartering their bodies for some affection

Men weak because life is hard

No wars to clean out the attic

No plagues to settle the score

Our battles are not spiritual

Stop fooling yourself

Everyone is enslaved by money.

Avenger

My bike weaves between parking spots

I am the night avenger

Secretly planning my route

Got to make my get away

Put the gear in neutral

I cut the engine

The key will remain in the ignition

I check my mirrors

Then left and right

One can never be too safe in this business

In a flash the deed is done

I am human again

I fade into the night

I don't even exist anyhow

But my spirit roams the streets

My bike - faithful iron horse

On we ride into the night

Next adventure awaits around the corner.

Brothers in arms

March on !

From the battle worn hills

Boots torn

In the mud

March on !

We suffer

We die

Under the grace of God

From parched clouds stream the sun

Men line up to march

Uncertain death awaits beyond the hills

Silently we march on

As the poppy flowers swing in the wind

Saying farewell

All these men will be history

A few tears shed

They will pass into the realm of forgetfulness

We know not what we fight for

What we die for

Yet angels of death wait for us beyond those hills

We shall embrace the ground

Our blood shall spill in red

Marking the hour of atonement

On a somber September morning

Those who live on will raise a flag in our honor

Forgotten

Erased from memories

We take our stand in the life beyond

Watching the turning of seasons

As a melancholic tune plays on

We all shall sing together as brothers in arms.

Visit

She comes to me in waves

I am the shore line

Timid

She advances only to retreat

She has paved a path

Sees no danger

Closer more intimate

She wants to be kissed

But I am the shore

Solid, firm

I stand my ground

She needs her assurances

Come to her own conclusions

Find her own reasons

That is why she visits to discover me

The boundaries she can fit in

Freedom to explore

Reasons to expand

Feel the ground solid beneath her feet

She is always elusive

Always uncertain

Finds her own comforting shores in my arms.

Predicament

Life is so fragile

Yet we all feel a sense of control

An illusion of our senses

Thinking we can direct the course of things

God must be laughing out loud

We are all fools grasping thin air

Lose your wealth, your boyfriend, your wife in an instant

Everything can take a turn for the worst in a day

Good things though build up slowly

Nothing surprises me

Birds in the trees are forever happy

Feed your cat she goes away

You are a beast don't you know ?

A monster in the making

Hoping, hoping, praying to your deities

Ha, ha, ha

You are probably the laughing stock of the universe

God is also laughing at your predicament.

Night of nights

Tonight I pray to you O'Lord

Creator of Heavens & Earth

May good prevail in my life

May I bring forth joy and happiness into my life and others

Give me the power to up lift people in my life

May I be wiser and more prudent each day

Know the right decisions

Have the courage to take them

Place powers in me to create beautiful things

Beyond all love be always present in me, around me

Forever

Amen

10 July 2015 Montreal

Pest

She is drunk

Sitting beside me

Her hair black blond

Lost soul

No answers at the bottom of the glass

But she does not know

She just repeats patterns

She got no story

A truck ran her down

She has been dead for men

Undesirable nuisance

A roach under the bed

No one bothers her anymore

She leaves saying

She is going to find her way home

Gone, she is gone

Vanish into the night

A mosquito hits the light bulb

Falls dead.

Paradise

You text me at 3.49 am

'Bonne Nuit'

What does that suppose to mean ?

After I have not heard from you in weeks

Why does the thought of me run through your mind ?

Did your latest fling had enough of you ?

Did you just feel lonely one night ?

When all my nights are lonely I am the addict for company

I am the disgrace among men who never gets to touch a woman's breast

My lips are dry because they have not been kissed in ages

I am the loneliest man in Montreal

Bums in the corner washing windshields even have girlfriends

Thousands of women will go to bed without anyone tonight

All I got are my words that have never been appreciated

What can a man give when no one is ready to receive ?

A woman walks in through my door one night

She says I am yours

Take me tonight

This man is in paradise.

She is 38

Well grounded

Have interests

She can hold a conversation

Do a number of things at the same time

She texts me

I am excited because

She likes me

Push a side the past

Be the courageous soul

Open your sails

Let wind blow into them

You are bound for a new destination

You are the ship un sunk

A weather beaten wane

Pointing towards hope

You are the clouds drifting on a beautiful day

Hold a woman in your arms

Be the sanctuary of the tenderest kisses.

Artists

I am sitting in a cafe

It is 10 in the morning

Someone is playing the piano

Another one got a cowboy hat

Plucking the string of a bass guitar

A quiet jazz vibe fills the air

My coffee tastes better

The book under my hand is now obsolete

Poetry is dead don't you know !

We are the dying breed of artists

Once we are gone

Talent would be a book topic

Words come easily

We feed from each other

Musician put their notes down

Painters come up with new ideas

Writers compose enchanting sentences

All this happens in a little cafe

Somewhere on Bernard street

Montreal still got the magic

She is sultry

I am drawn to her

She kisses me in the mouth

And I am in love once again.

Brothers

We share food

We are the monks of the world

Miners in deep dark crevices of the earth

Soldiers tired from fighting till dusk

We break bread in the biblical sense

Part with ourselves

Share with our hearts

We are love in the twilight

Brothers entrusted through life.

Dead silence

I wait for the night

That is when dead silence comes

When I can hear my breath

Even the mosquitoes on the ceiling have a hum

Then I begin writing

Mostly about the most random things

Because at this hour

Everything is a sleep

Not even the leaves on the trees make a move

It is just me, alone tonight

My words keep me company

Here we wait silently

All the creatures of the night and I

We are nocturnal beings

Feeling, breathing, thinking

Because there is nothing else to do

Then just when we are convinced that nothing could ever happen

This poem is born.

Asylum

I am seated where Leonard Cohen once used to sit

In this joint his afternoons used to pass

He is gone now

This place has not changed since

There is no linger scent of his cigarettes

But his ghost is still here

Eking out an existence

Depressed as always

Only Hydra could save him

Then even that is over

He is off in some place in LA

Content to be passing his days with his lover

His words though hang in the air

All the agitation, frustration still echoes on the walls here

I am here to build the asylum

Where he left off

Complete the circle

Listen... 'poems from Montreal' is coming

You will hear from me.

13 July 2015 Montreal

Written in "Main Restaurant"

Legacy

What are you doing here ?

Don't you know it is 6 in the morning ?

You always slept till noon

A woman who could waste her hours away

And now you are bothering me,

Your presence,

Thoughts of you are swirling in my head,

Half my bed is empty,

You crazy thing,

Don't you know we are through ?

You have taken your marbles and left for greener pastures

You who thought life would be better without me

Looked for ways out of our relationship

Now you do as you please

You would never call me

Like all the good men who could have meant something

As you said to every men who said to you 'I love you'

You replied 'but I don't'

That is your story

That is your legacy

Now I am left here

Going to stab at all our memories

One day I will slay my love

Then there would be no poems for you

Then you would be dead to me.

15 July 2015 Montreal

Hole in the ceiling

I stare at walls

There is a hole in the ceiling

Where the light gets in

It shines upon me

I am motionless

I am taken,

captivated by this feeling

Overwhelmed I say nothing

Words become feathers suspended in mid air

Weightless seconds stall

Time stretches to eternity

It is magic unfolding

And I am speechless

Love just pierced through my skin.

Waiting

I am waiting

For breakfast

For lunch

In lines I am standing

For coffee

For my turn to speak

At the stop sign in the corner

To have luck go my way

I am waiting

Crazy ideas pop in my head

Words sprinkled with magic dust appear

Poems fill the empty space

Stories are created instantaneously

Dreams are dreamth

While I am waiting

In the end

I can't wait anymore

I am creating.

Ghost

She comes as a ghost

Gracefully moving across my house

She is here to be a witness

Indulge in some earthly pleasures

She drinks the wine

Eats the food

She is among the mortals

But for a day

Tomorrow she will be no more

Disappear

That is what she says she is good at

Then mentions walking

As Jesus must have walked on water

In some miraculous way

Will walk through tonight among us

Then she will be no more

No more pretty white dress

Bare feet kissing the floor

She was here for sure

A ghost indulging in mortal pleasures

A hug before she disappeared into the night

I am left with faint memories of her

A pair of eyes so deep

I am lost in them.

Poetry prize

It is quiet in the park

Sun is gently making her presence

A cross the benches sits a fat man topless basking in her rays

I am munching on dark red cherries

Coffee besides me

I am working through some Bukowski

Among poets I may be the last of them

Now poetry is in the hands of the academician

They are dissecting phrases

Putting prosthetic meanings

All the while looking at everything with contempt

I am the outcast

No fine decorated doctorate degree

No one should mention that the apartheid is dead

She is well alive in the halls of universities

Published scholarly magazines

Most likely my books will never be read

I have not won any poetry prizes

I could not careless if a poetry magazine publishes my poem

A crazy woman sits at another bench

She seems totally content talking to herself

I better be quiet now.

Prayer

Early morning

I only hear the rustling of the leaves

A sky in light blue cloak rests upon me

I am as I have been before

Peaceful, serene, patient

Solitude is as Rilke has said is

A blessing

Here and now

My words come one by one

Through a mysterious eternal force

Holy Spirit moves me

Gods have commanded

So shall be written

However insignificant my words are

I shall not question

I am only the vessel

Writing, composing, grateful

This is the opening

Through which love receives light

Graceful, serene, peaceful

I am held together by the Divine

This is my prayer.

Sleep chasing

Here is the impossible

At 7.21 am

After another sleepless night

I am welcoming morning

Call me foolish if you wish

But I am worried about being worried

Keeps me awake

Try telling yourself to go to sleep

Wide open eyes staring at the ceiling

Hours keep passing by

I am on a train somewhere in Europe

Green fields are going by

Try sleeping

Taking some sleep medication

After 3 days it does not work

At 220 km an hour

This train is heading south

Would we be crossing the Italian border ?

May be I would end up on a beach somewhere

Dipping my feet in the water

Try sleeping now

I am day dreaming

Some cute girl starts talking to me about art

Have I seen Michelangelo's David ?

They say it is quiet daunting

I must be dashing because

I am in Rome in some piazza

Having dinner with the love of my life

Have you seen what time it is ?

We are already past 4 am

Would you know if the next stop is Rome ?

Some conductor told me that the train is bound for Amalfi

I should be there

Have I been sleeping on the way ?

Seriously try going to sleep

I hear you can take some blue pill for that

But I am afraid I will miss all this

You would not want me to miss all this would you ?

Your beautiful legs

Us making love in our bed

Oh, apologies

Have I been day dreaming again ?

I see the times is 6.30 am

How convenient !

Now I got the sun coming in

Sleep, sleep

Have you got a lullaby for me ?

Like the ones my mother used to sing to me

You know I would love to lay my head on your lap

While you play with my hair in some Greek island

I can smell the sea

Would we be having croissants this morning ?

Do you remember the time when we were in Paris ?

How you pretended to be happy

Even you believed it

Now it is past 7

I must be going

I have got some catching up with sleep now

But before I go

Will you give me a kiss like the one you gave me in Marmaris ?

Later on we could be making love

While Depeche Modes "in your room" plays on

Oh, I am sorry

You just reminded me that you could be having sex for 8 hours straight

But I don't rank in the list

Because you never loved me

Bonne nuit my dear

I am in Montreal

Perhaps you'd remember our days here

MDMA and Hernan mixed in between

I am sure you are happy pursuing new love affairs

I must be going now

Sleep awaits

I know you are already on your way

You just could not stand me

I am standing in line for some sleep

While my mind rings

Bon matin.. Bon matin..

First date

I will have my coffee

Then be on my way

Any hour any day

My life can change for the better

She awaits

At 10 am

It could be amazing

She - walking out of her apartment

Smiling

An exchange of niceties

We are driving together

Excitement of a first date

Immense possibilities

A man, a woman

The world is our oyster.

Making movies

Four guys in a car

We shuffled in

Hardly any room to move

I am taking a deep breath in

Something just got to click

My eyes are heavy

Drifting ever deep

Got to find the bottom

Filming a scene

This is how the movies are made

Everyone does something

Hoping all turns out good

Fair to say we live on prayers

Our business is make believe

Illusions of reality

That is what dreams are made of

We call it making movies.

Recoleta

A big fat steak sits on my plate

I am transported to Argentina

A story that can't be told

Patagonia, tango, Palermo

Dazzle me, enchant me

I am already a poet

Give me more wine (mozo mas copa)

I hear Cumparsita

I hear Pugliese whispering in my ear

Don't you know I am buried in Recoleta ?

I have got some musician friends here

I hear Gardel singing

You see I am enchanted

A steak takes be back

And I am in love with a beautiful Argentinean woman

She loves me

Her eyes pierce me

I am helpless

I love her

But I am guilty

Because I betrayed love

Turned the bed on Death

She haunts me at night

I still carry the burden of a broken heart

I am a sparrow

Broken

My voice is no more

But my spirit lives on

I left my foot prints in a milonga

I desire her

But I am dead

Buried in Recoleta

She haunts me to love her

I whisper

I still love you

You boil my blood

Your eyes pierce

I am wounded for love

Because of love

Of you I speak

I am in love till eternity.

4.37 in the morning

I hear the gentle drops of rain on leaves outside my window

At 4.37 in the morning

I am part of the silence broken by the rain's caress

I am the fragility of small things

Unbroken by heart's desires

I wish only to be there

Ever so silent

Hidden

I am here to be a witness

Of the beauty

Gentle rain drops on leaves outside my window

Caressing of one thing upon the other

All is beautiful

All is here

I am the witness at 4.37 in the morning.

Mad woman

She accuses me of things

I can only laugh

Her insanity for a man half a continent away

She plays the victim

Compulsive behavior of trying to contact him

What beautiful story for a film

Woman gone mad

For a love she never had

She slit her wrists in the bath tub

Only her diaries and poems remain

Discovered early on Sunday morning

By a concerned neighbor

It had been 3 weeks since she was last seen

Tragedy of a human life had ended.

Nothing kills

Call me

I am lonely tonight

It is not because I miss you

I just need you to be here

Because nothing kills loneliness

You are my weakness

Quenching my thirst for human interaction

I have not touched a woman's skin

Not for the longest time

That is why I am lonely tonight

I just need you to be here

Because my skin misses you

I can lie saying I am fine

I don't need anyone

But nothing kills loneliness in the middle of the night.

Perfect life

Sun washes me gently

There are pretty girls around

Life is a bliss

Just like a dream

Never want to wake up

Pause time here

Make the moment last forever

This is happiness

I am suspended in the present

The girl tells me that her name is Esma

That she is from France

A lie - a slap to awaken me

I return to reality

She ignores me

Happy to be talking to a nerdy twenty year old

I knock my coffee

Cut my hand

Life is as it should once again.

The poet

Early hours of the morning

I am awake to witness

The dawning of a new day

When everything will be alive

I will gaze with the eyes of a child

To life, love and beyond

I am the poet translating

Emotions into phrases

Action into words

I am the distiller

Bringing forth the essence of the moment

Mediating in the presence of life

I am love undefined

A caresser of human soul

I am the poet speaking to your beauty.

Witness

All awaits

Daunting tasks

Impossible missions

Prayers for a breakthrough

Dreams of a better tomorrow

I stare at the sky blindly

White puffy clouds moving through

Sunshines ever so brightly

I am complacent

I am absorbed in the moment

I breath the summer

Green luscious grass

Flowers on trees

Girls in shorts

I am still

Observing

A witness

A life passes before my eyes

And I smile.

Rage

3.23 am I am drifting in time

Is it morning or night ?

Shades of the dark play shadows

The moon is washing the streets of my city

And I am alone again

No one in my bed

I lay here dreaming

A film, poetry, something must come out

I have been cornered

Things have bottled up in me

A volcanic eruption

A furious rage

I promise I burn all my bridges

I stand on top of a hill

And see my past burn in a haze

I laugh with contentment

Fulfilled my dream.

Love left

I can't stop

Not for you

Not for me

I am a speeding bullet train

An arrow that has left the bow

Nothing comes back anyway

Not the words we have spoken

Not the love we have destroyed

I am the shrapnel piercing through flesh

I am the sadness that pulls the gun's trigger

I am destiny head on

Nothing holds me back

Your love has left me.

Life calling

My heart is pounding

I am breathless

Standing still

Reality is over bearing

I am by the window

Sun shines outside

Calling me to play

I hear, I hear

Life's saying

'You have been here before

Now take wings and fly

You have got dreams

Hopes & wishes to fulfill'

Then all is well

I write this poem

Saying thank you.

Made man

Keeps on ticking

Minutes, seconds

There is no escape

It is just me and inevitability

We stare at each other in the face

Who shall flinch

Who shall take a step back

I am here to prove myself

Destiny is at hand

At 43 a man has a choice to make

Create something grand or

Die living for a dream

Now we have a ticking time

Inevitability is at hand

We have got to make it through this

Be a man who has made it.

Line

We are lined up

Waiting for our turns

This is just us

Servants of time

We stand and wait

Ordinary day while life waits out there

We kill time for our turn

We are the slaves of a system

Between work and sleep

We attempt to live

Passing time in lines and traffic

We are all lined up for our turns

One day we will begin to live.

A new beginning

Another day

Sun is up

Asking me if I want to play

Ride my motorcycle down some country road

Eat at a small diner

It is like a new beginning

De ja vu of places I have been

Things I have forgotten

Your kiss

Smell of your skin

Freshly mowed grass

Leaves turning green

Some strange place I have never been

It is a new beginning.

As earth loves rain

Clouds move in

Sun is hidden

Soon will come the down pour

I stand ready as a tree

Waiting for my leaves to be soaked

My roots shall be quenched

I will bathe in your glorious rain

I shall sprout new branches

Send my roots deeper

My leaves will spread closer to the sky

I shall be closer to you

Touching your breath

Listening to your melody

My leaves will sing to your glory

Come closer to me

Caress me with your blessing

I shall love you as earth loves rain.

Bliss

Floating in happiness

Blissful womb

I return to where I began

I am swimming in a dream

Everything is perfect

Sky blue marry the golden sun

I am cast into a spell

I see you and know you are mine

It is sacred, sublime, supreme

Heaven this must be

Reality is just a nightmare.

Busy

You tell me you are busy

You can't see me

Isn't life tough ?

Is if we have not got enough

You keep your distance

We skillfully kill feelings

Not knowing why

We become lonely

Calling out for someone to save us

Darling, we create our own hell

Make love the first thing

So we may be together

I hear loneliness can leave us.

A song

Write me a song

With a melody that shall resonate beyond time

Tell me story that moves me closer to you

Sing a tune

That shall dwell in my heart

Do it so love shall be me

We be the love

You whisper your secrets

That we may know each other

Bind us in eternity

Like no beginning and no end

That we may become the song of the Creator

We unite in his presence

Be one in all things.

At rest

I have stopped

This is the moment of rest

Body seizes motion

My brain is still racing

My breath still heavy

I have to surrender

Accept my faith

I am standing at the edge

Still, quiet, motionless

Waiting the void to engulf me

This is what it means to be serene

Face death and don't flinch

Stare him in the eye

Show him that I am not afraid

He has not come to take me

I am still questioning

If I should take him by the hand anyway

Then he is gone

I am laying in my bed

Naked, helpless, still

Typing away this

I have been dead

Resurrected and reborn

I follow Faith

She just takes me.

Change

I am waiting for my steak

I have changed

I am a different man now

My potato arrives stuffed with everything

I can't say I know the new person in this body

He is living for today

Does not care about tomorrow

I am eating my steak

That is what he chose

An indulgence into senses

Living this day is if it is our last day.

Dream

Eleni Karaindrou is playing

Music is in my head

I can't listen with my ears

My skull is the acoustic walls of the concert hall

I am staring into dead space

Numbness spreads through me

I don't feel anything or

I am overwhelmed

Does it matter ?

She does not mean anything

What a lie !

I am writing poems still

I find her in everything

Mundane little things have her hidden

She haunts me

I may never be free again

Fall in love with another woman

That is the dream.

Goddess

I sit by your window

You are ever so beautiful

Moving between your things

Your make up, clothes and shoes

Goddess of a beautiful facade

Your smile charms the soul

Mortals fall victim

Men lured by a fantasy of being with you

Loving you eternally

At their most vulnerable moment

You just wave them off

Is if they never mattered at all

You are the Goddess

Pretension

A disguise of spiritual search

Sweetest lie of lived happily ever after

Mask of a merciless executioner

Death of hope

Love obscured

You are all alone

You have been fooled.

Futon

She throws out the futon

She says it reminds her of x boyfriend

I am carrying it down the stair

Memories carried out of her life

Futon is gone

She forgets him

Simple as that

Hands washed clean

Done with the past

Sometime life can be that easy.

Diplomacy

He comes in

Sits at the corner of my studio

There is no escape

We are bound to go through this

Explanations, reasonings, excuses

This is what we need to see

Reality in extremes,

Frustration, defeat,

A delicate balance of diplomacy

There are no winners in this game

We are here to sacrifice things

Then one of us yields

Climax is reached

We reel back fast

Salvage our spirits

Praise each other

Is if nothing happened here.

Fragile thing

Waiting

Waiting for the inevitable

Decay of the body

Loss of senses

Slowing of reflexes

In between there is hope

Encased in a fanus

Fragile

I stare at it

She is glorious

Illuminated by my spirit

I am enchanted

She just waits

Waits to be free

When I set her free

We no longer have to wait

Hope shall leave me

For now though she is my only companion

I dream of her

She is a prisoner of my dreams

She waits for me to be ready

Then she will leave me

And we both will be happy.

Flower fields

We are aging men

Gazing at flowers fields & orchards

We want to indulge

Get lost in carnal pleasures

Feast with Dionysus

Seated at his right

Taste the flesh of tender fruit

Smell the freshly blossomed flowers

Celebrate life

And be in awe of ourselves

That we can still do this.

Crescent moon

A fire burns in the backyard

Friends have gathered around

Someone plays a guitar

Under the crescent moon

We are happy

We sing songs

Time becomes a far far away story.

Our voices rise high towards the sky

We are close to heaven

As the crescent moon lingers between the clouds

Night is written in the stars

Shining bright with our laughters

We make love with our most intimate part

As the crescent moon enchants.

Lady bug

You plump thing

Dreaming of finding a lover

Search, search high 'n low

Between work and bed

You believe you find a man

Drink, drink your wine

Fat aging lady bug.

Hunt

We are seasoned hunters

Not as fast as we used to be

Our faces show our years

We sniff opportunity

Plan an angle of attack

Approach our prey gently

Speak ever softly

Allow our ease with words

Lull our target to comfort

Then at a precise moment

Right question is posed

Numbers are exchanged

She is game.

Innocence

Collecting things

Dropping them as I go along

Greedy lust for experience

I am counting on my creativity

Dreaming of bigger things

Kisses in endless nights

Feeling the sand beneath my feet

Forgetting everything

Loving with the innocence of a child.

.

Sleep

Sleep calls

It is past midnight

An early hour for bed

Yet I follow her

She does not like to be refused

Insistent on getting her way

She whispers to me sweetly

I follow

Before I awake I know

It will be a new day tomorrow.

Kiss

I hear Japanese pop songs here

Reminds me of my days in Japan

Have I been in a dream ?

Does anything I eat here take me back ?

I am the blossom of the cherry tree

I am the wading moon on a summer night

I am the ever changing colors of the leaves

Yet I stand here remembering yesterday

Am I not but a day ?

Can you kiss me to remind me that your love is real ?

25 June 2015 Montreal

Written at Kobusa Izikaya restaurant

Lament

I walk through the streets of Montreal

I see reminders of you

A mural in an alley

A wheat paste on a back door

Footsteps we had taken together

A ghost of you walks with me

Enchanted I follow

In the mazes of mind I get lost

Was it real or a dream ?

Were we happy ever ?

It does not matter now

You have moved on

Would not remember anything here

I never meant anything to you anyway

So why I lament ?

Prayer

When there is no more to give shall I receive ?

If I pray would I be a good man ?

I have been lost you know

I am the lamb that wandered off the flock

Now there is a chance that history may be rewritten

If I am among the white sheep again some day

My black coat will stand beautiful

Praises shall rise to the Glorious One

What shall happen to you remains to be seen

You in your sanctuary of comfort

What would the Lord say for you have played love for fool

Is there no retribution for a mad woman ?

Go on walk your path

You never appreciated what you had

Be the love bug that lands on many flesh

I long to see how all this ends.

Mornings

Each morning I get up with thoughts of you

Some little memory of us

I am a prisoner of my mind

Thinking of you incessantly

That is how I go crazy

Very slowly, excruciatingly painfully

There are no walls here

Just a prison where

I count the hours and days until I am free

In the mean time I wait

Burning the long hours of nights with poems I write

Days trying to forget you

Analyzing the reasons

Remembering the unimportant

It is madness creeping upon me

Obsession built upon thoughts

I am a prisoner without walls

Dying slowly

In the end life kills all.

That is life

Argentinian radio on

I am listening

Reminiscing for a love I left behind in Buenos Aires

She loved me

I just could not be around

I ran away to the other end of the world

My soul is tormented

My heart twisted

Ashes of a love still burns in me

I think of her sometimes

May be we meet someday I say

Life would have passed us by then

We will cry,

Consul ourselves for all those lost years

That is life my love

That is life what can I say.

Cuteness

You with your beautiful smile

Your flesh ever so white

I am the madness under the illusion

Cuteness that is what you are

A porcelain doll

Ever so precious

You are never owned or loved

You are the monster beneath the sea

A disaster in the midst of a dream

An earth shattering experience

A tornado has left

Ruins of hope

Patched up lives

Constructed on damp soil

You sink beneath everything

Nothing is spared

Only destruction remains.

Mistral

Rain falls outside my window

Melancholic day

Smell of wet streets

Sound of splashing puddles

I reminiscence about our summer

Sun, blue Mediterranean sea

Lazy hours spent together

All gone, part of history

Fragile love extinguished

Mistrals are no more

We both live with the consequence now.

Rain's story

Rain seems everywhere

The streets are soaked

My windows are covered in raindrops

Grey clouds tell their story

I am deaf I don't want to hear

No thunders, no lightning

Just a dull day without a voice

I want to see fireflies

Stars in the sky

A smile after a kiss

A whisper in bed

A promise to love

Even if it is for a day

That is what I tell rain.

Zombie

She is horrific

The way she stands there and delivers

Her lies, deception and tricks

We are all vulnerable

She makes you think she is the sweetest pretty thing

You are her victim

Crimes, skeletons in her closet

She just would not care

Murder in cold blood

Not shed a single tear

She just got a thick skin

No nerve endings

Nor any guilt trips

Suppressed emotions

She is devil's best friend

She pretends she can love

But ends up playing black widow

Go on smell the deadly flower

Bite into the poisoned apple

You are going to die some day

Now you are just a living zombie.

Life is

I am afraid

That is normal

I am on the edge

Worried about tomorrow

That is not what life is

Wide open green fields

A lover's kiss upon your lips

Gratitude for another day of living

Is not that what life is ?

Com'on get up

Com'on get up

This is the moment

Are you awake ?

Has life left you behind ?

Speak to me

Let me hear you yell

For all the hurt, suffering and disappointment

You have got to be someone

Got to fight your war

Victory is the only true thing to be proud of

There is no glory in poverty

Achievements are but marks of souls.

A friend

Avocado, toasted bread

Simple few things

Conversation with a friend

Over a meal,

Laughter hits the walls,

We are of men same age,

Remembering great days of yester years,

Speaking the same language,

Having lost pretty much everything

We hold fast to our hopes for better days.

Banquet

There is always a cause for celebration

Weddings, engagements, graduations

We are the voyeurs in attendance

Not part of anything

Just decoration for friends

We mingle, provide entertainment

Harmless bodies in a sea of people

We smile and make pleasant conversation

Useful nuisance of our necessary presence bring delight to any party.

Invite us we will be there for your celebration

Our value is indispensable.

The pick up

Women are everywhere,

We are the aged wolf pack,

Some simple question

Then the show begins

I stay back and let my friend speak

He is refined to lead the conversation

Soon phone numbers are exchanged

A coffee date is set in our milieu

That is the agreement

A finesse through repeated story telling

Women respond to my friend

I am rusty

Not up to speed,

It is the show I must watch and learn

I have been single too long

God is helping me to get back on my feet.

Life of excellence

This could be a life changing moment

My meeting with this friend

He shows me where I need to improve

My failures become successes

I learn new things

Become a better version of myself

What has eluded me all my life

Is no longer a mystery

Finally the circle is complete

My life balanced on a scale

I see everything as perfection

I keep honing my skills

Say this is my masterpiece

A life lived in excellence.

Victory

3 am

Dead of the night

I am awake on a warm summer night

I now just wait

It is a struggle

A wrestling match between

Two foes

My worries keeping me awake

Exhaustion pulling me to slumber

Who wins tonight ?

Do I see the morning light or quietly fall asleep ?

I write because I must

It is the only way to fight the madness

My words form poems

My worries weaken

It is an allegiance with exhaustion

Tonight I pray for sleep

A victory for me.

What life is

I am afraid

That is normal

I am at the edge

Worried about tomorrow

That is not what life is

Wide open green fields

Wind in your hair

Kiss of a lover upon your lip

Laying down to sleep with gratitude for another day of living

Is not that what life is ?

Life's secrets

Sun shines over my shoulder,

It is a perfect afternoon,

I am an observer in awe

Experiencing life's unfolding before my eyes

My mind is racing

So much just comes in

The wind, the sound of the leaves on trees, the chatter of nearby strangers,

Shadows and lights mingle,

All so sweet,

I am in the womb of rebirth

I see all things naked

I want to kiss the sun

Dance with the wind

Take wings with birds in the sky

Be the melody in a lover's voice

I want to be love

And melt into a woman's heart

Touch the tenderest part of your soul.

Give you wings

Take you higher than the clouds

Show you the deepest ecstasy in life's secrets

Then fold you in my bosom

And caress you like a child

Hold you as a mother would her baby

Give you love

So you may grow.

Life fleeting

Life is fleeting

Moments come and go

My breath uneven

My eyes darken

Vision blurred

Medication don't help

Life is fleeting

Memories flash before my eyes

Hard to breath now

I am weakened

Words escape me

Death leave me be !

My suffering is the bread

While life is still in my veins

I shall feast upon pain

Life shall return to me.

Exile

I am stranded

Lost in a continent

I suppose this is called pain

Loneliness, struggle, exile

I am just waiting

I have made a choice

Now there is no going back

A fight for survival

A desire to live

With pain or without remorse

However it may be

I miss the bosom of my mother

Love of my lover

It is called loneliness

No, I am not bitter

This life teaching me to live again.

Printed in October 2021
by Rotomail Italia S.p.A., Vignate (MI) - Italy